TAKE TEN YEARS

1920s

Library of Congress Cataloging-in-Publication Data

Sharman, Margaret.
    1920s / written by Margaret Sharman.
        p.   cm. — (Take ten years)
    Includes index.
    Summary: Explores the decade of the 1920s worldwide, a time which included the formation of the League of Nations, Prohibition, the discovery of the tomb of Tutankhamun, Lindbergh's transatlantic flight, and the stock market crash.
    ISBN 0-8114-3075-8
    1. History, Modern—20th century—Juvenile literature.
    [1. History, Modern—20th century.]   I. Title.   II. Title: Nineteen twenties.   III. Series.
D720.S48   1992   92-17526
909.82—dc20   CIP
                                                         AC

Typeset by Multifacit Graphics, Keyport, NJ
Printed in Spain by GRAFO, S.A., Bilbao
Bound in the United States by Lake Book, Melrose Park, IL
1 2 3 4 5 6 7 8 9 0 LB 97 96 95 94 93 92

Acknowledgments

Maps — Jillian Luff of Bitmap Graphics
Design — Neil Sayer
Editor — Caroline Sheldrick

For permission to reproduce copyright material the author and publishers gratefully acknowledge the following:

Cover photographs — Historic New Orleans Collection; Bettmann; Brown Brothers; The Hulton Picture Company; Culver Pictures

page 4 — (from top) Mary Evans Picture Library, Mary Evans Picture Library, Popperfoto, Popperfoto; Page 5 — (top) The Hulton Picture Company, (others) Mary Evans Picture Library; page 9 — (left) The Hulton Picture Company, (right) UPI/Bettmann; page 10 — (top) Brown Brothers, (bottom) The Vintage Magazine Co; page 11 — (left) Brown Brothers, (right) The Hulton Picture Company; page 12 — (top) Culver Pictures, Inc., (bottom) The Hulton Picture Company; page 13 — Topham; page 14 — (top) The Bettmann Archive, (center) The Vintage Magazine Co., (bottom) Western History Collections, University of Oklahoma Library; page 15 — The Bettmann Archive; page 16 — (top and bottom right) The Hulton Picture Company, (bottom left) Topham; page 17 — Popperfoto; page 18 — (top) Culver Pictures, Inc., (bottom) The Bettmann Archive; page 19 — Brown Brothers; page 20 — (top) The Vintage Magazine Co., (bottom) Topham; page 21 — (top) Topham, (center) ECOSCENE, (bottom) Mary Evans Picture Library; page 22 — (center) Brown Brothers (right) The Hulton Picture Company, (bottom) The Vintage Magazine Co.; page 23 — UPI/Bettmann; page 24 — (top) Brown Brothers, (bottom) All-Sport Photographic Ltd; page 25 — (center) Topham, (bottom), e.t. archive; page 27 — The Vintage Magazine Co; page 28 — Bridgeman Art Library, London; page 29 — Mary Evans Picture Library; page 30 — Brown Brothers; page 31 — (top left and center) Brown Brothers, (bottom) Topham; page 32 — The Vintage Magazine Co.; page 33 — (top and center) Topham, (bottom) The Vintage Magazine Co.; page 34 — (top) Brown Brothers, (center) The Hulton Picture Company, (bottom) Topham; page 35 — Mary Evans Picture Library; page 36 — Popperfoto; page 37 — (left) The Bettmann Archive, (bottom) Popperfoto; page 38 — (top) Popperfoto, (center) The Vintage Magazine Co.; page 39 — Popperfoto; page 40 — The Vintage Magazine Co.; page 41 — The Hulton Picture Company; page 42 — (left) UPI/Bettmann, (right) National Portrait Gallery, Smithsonian Institution, Washington, D.C.; page 43 — (top) Culver Pictures, Inc., (center) Popperfoto, (bottom) The Hulton Picture Company; page 44 — The Advertising Archives; page 45 — The Advertising Archives; (last picture) The Vintage Magazine Company.

TAKE TEN YEARS

1920s

MARGARET SHARMAN

RSVP
**RAINTREE
STECK-VAUGHN**
P U B L I S H E R S
The Steck-Vaughn Company

Austin, Texas

Contents

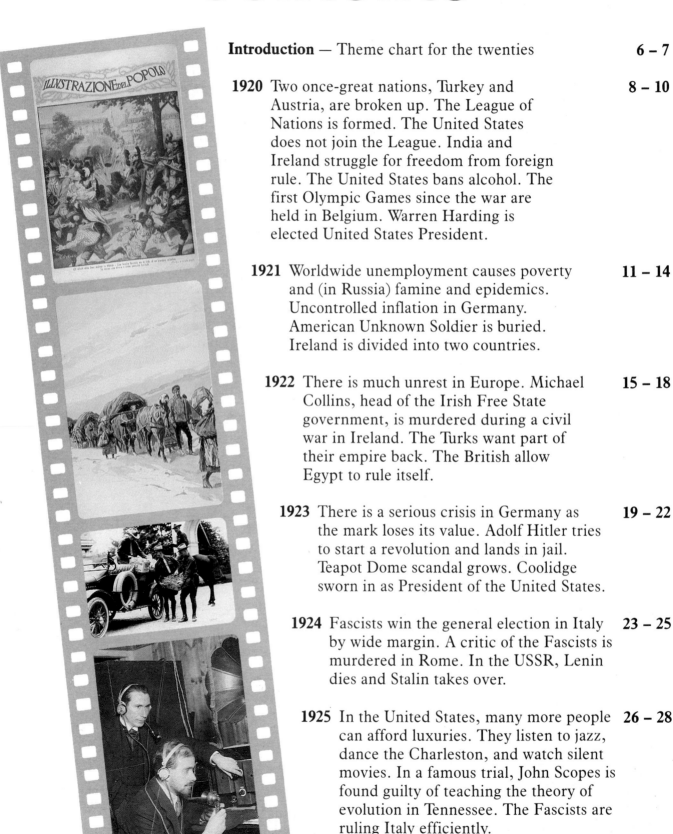

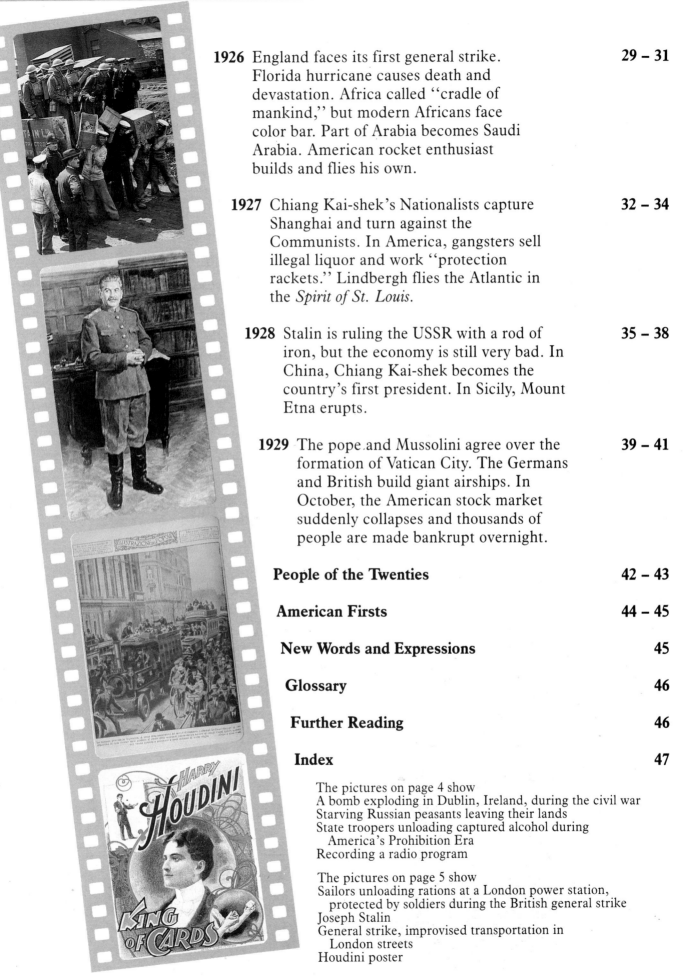

The pictures on page 4 show
A bomb exploding in Dublin, Ireland, during the civil war
Starving Russian peasants leaving their lands
State troopers unloading captured alcohol during
   America's Prohibition Era
Recording a radio program

The pictures on page 5 show
Sailors unloading rations at a London power station,
   protected by soldiers during the British general strike
Joseph Stalin
General strike, improvised transportation in
   London streets
Houdini poster

Introduction

After World War I (then called the Great War), European countries had to rebuild everything: their homes, their industries, and even their lives. Men returning from the war found no work. First the factories and the shops had to be rebuilt, and markets found for their products.

Almost every European country was affected. Before the war, Turkey and Austria had large empires. Both fought on the losing side, and after the war the countries they had occupied became new small nations. These nations had to learn to manage their own affairs. In Germany and Italy, the standard of living was very low after the war. New political parties, the Nazis and the Fascists, took over the weak governments there.

In America, women had the vote, and some had jobs. Their clothing showed that they no longer stayed at home all day — skirts were shorter and more practical for walking in the streets or catching a bus. The huge hats they used to wear were gone and would never come back.

To forget the gloom of the war years young people went to "tea dances," where they danced the Charleston. It was fashionable to smoke cigarettes through long, thin cigarette holders, and drink cocktails. They listened to jazz. The lucky ones owned a wireless set.

In the United States, alcohol was banned, but it was not difficult to get "bootleg" gin (so called because in the old days smugglers hid bottles in their seaboots, and were known as "bootleggers"). The country was very prosperous, and Americans were loving their new wealth. They bought huge houses. They gave parties. They drove Model T Fords or Chevrolets. They swooned over Rudolph Valentino in his movie *The Sheikh*. They invested their new wealth in stocks and shares, and the profits went up and up. Then, right at the end of the decade, the stock market collapsed. Shares were worth nothing. The unbelievable had happened; the Great Depression began on both sides of the Atlantic.

YEARS	WORLD AFFAIRS
1920	Turkey and Austria lose their empires.
1921	Germany: the Reparations Bill Widespread unemployment Anglo-Irish Treaty
1922	Egypt becomes a kingdom. Italy has a Fascist government. Turks threaten the Dardanelles.
1923	Economic crisis in Germany Russia becomes the USSR. French occupy the Ruhr.
1924	Stalin begins to take over leadership of USSR.
1925	Italy becomes a dictatorship. Prosperity in U.S.A.
1926	General strike in Britain Kingdom of Saudi Arabia recognized.
1927	Nationalists challenge Communists in China.
1928	Stalin is in full control of USSR.
1929	Stock market crashes. Creation of Vatican City Mustafa Kemal's reforms in Turkey

WARS & CIVIL DISORDER	PEOPLE	EVENTS
Civil war in Ireland	Gandhi emerges as Indian nationalist. Harding becomes U.S. President. U.S. women vote in national election.	League of Nations begins work. Prohibition of alcohol in U.S.A. Olympic Games in Antwerp
Race riot in Tulsa, Oklahoma	Enrico Caruso dies. Sacco and Vanzetti convicted of murder. Banting and Best discover insulin.	First "Miss America" beauty competition America's unknown soldier buried.
The IRA splits into two parties, which fight each other. End of war between Turkey and Greece Civil disobedience in India	Michael Collins, head of Irish Free State, shot dead. Mussolini leads Italy's Fascists.	New pope elected. *Reader's Digest* started. Annie Oakley breaks shooting record. Pharaoh Tutankhamun's tomb found.
Ku Klux Klan active in southern states of U.S.A.	Röntgen, Nobel Prize winner, dies. Coolidge becomes U.S. President on death of Harding.	U.S. Army pilots to fly non-stop coast-to-coast. Earthquake in Japan Howard University bans discrimination. President Harding dies.
	Miriam Ferguson becomes first woman to be elected a U.S. governor. Schweitzer rebuilds hospital in West Africa. Mateotti, Mussolini's critic, murdered. Coolidge elected President.	Olympic Games in Paris Will Rogers opens in Ziegfield Follies. Lenin dies.
	Carter reveals Tutankhamun's mummy. F. Scott Fitzgerald publishes *The Great Gatsby*. Hitler publishes *Mein Kampf.*	Duke University in North Carolina becomes richest in the U.S. through tobacco tycoon's will. Darwin's evolution theory on trial in U.S.A. Chaplin movie *The Gold Rush* released.
	American Gertrude Ederle is first woman to swim English Channel. Death of actor Rudolph Valentino	Ancient skull found in South Africa. Powerful hurricane strikes Florida. Buried city found in Yucatán.
Chiang Kai-shek opposes China's warlords.	American violinist, 11-year-old Yehudi Menuhin, delights European audiences. Drinker and Shaw completing iron lung Baseball hero "Babe" Ruth scores record number of runs. Lindbergh flies Atlantic.	First talking picture, *The Jazz Singer*, released.
Chinese and Japanese clash.	Walt Disney creates Mickey Mouse. Campbell breaks land speed record. Herbert Hoover is elected U.S. President.	Amelia Earhart flies Atlantic. Olympic Games in Amsterdam Mount Etna erupts.
	President Hoover signs bill to help U.S. farmers.	St. Valentine's Day massacre in U.S.A. Airship flies around the world. U.S. stock market crashes.

1920

A NEW INTERNATIONAL ORGANIZATION

Feb. 11, London Forty-two countries have become members of a new League of Nations. The Great War ended only 15 months ago, and the members hope to stop such wars in the future.

The League will ask the major powers to help support smaller or weaker countries. These countries will be called "mandates." Many of the countries that will become mandates were once part of the Turkish and Austrian empires, which have now been broken up.

There is much disappointment that America has so far refused to join the League.

TURKEY HAS LOST ITS EMPIRE

Aug. 10, Sèvres, France By a new treaty, Greece has won a large part of the old Turkish Empire. Hejaz in Arabia is now an independent country. Syria has already become a mandate of France; Mesopotamia and Palestine are new British mandates. The Dardanelles, where heavy fighting took place during the war, has been made an international zone. British, French, and Italian troops are guarding it.

HUNGARY'S BORDERS SHRINK

June 4, Versailles, France Hungary has been part of the Austrian Empire for 50 years. Now the northern area, where the Czechs and Slovaks live, will become Czechoslovakia. The southern part will be united with Yugoslavia. Hungary, with its capital at Budapest, is now less than a third of its size before the war.

A VOICE AGAINST THE EMPIRE

Sept. 10, Delhi Mr. Mohandas Gandhi, a young Indian lawyer who trained in Britain, wants the British to leave India. He suggests that Indians stop cooperating with them. They will not import British textiles, but will spin and weave their own.

HUNGARY'S NEW BORDERS

ESTONIA
LATVIA
LITHUANIA
Danzig
POLAND
RUSSIA
GERMANY
CZECHOSLOVAKIA
BESSARABIA
SWITZ.
AUSTRIA
HUNGARY
TRANSYLVANIA
YUGOSLAVIA
ROMANIA
ITALY
Black Sea
BULGARIA
ALBANIA
TURKEY
GREECE

0   mi   300

Old Austro-Hungarian Empire
— · — Post 1920 boundaries

PROHIBITION BRINGS CRIME

May 30, Chicago On January 16 it became illegal to buy or drink alcohol in any American state. Already "Prohibition" has led to illegal trade in alcohol. Crooks have realized that they can make big money by importing it illegally. These "bootleggers" give the police big bribes to "look the other way." Most citizens also turn a blind eye because they want to go on buying whiskey and gin.

CIVIL WAR FLARES UP IN IRELAND

Dec. 23, Ireland The Catholic nationalist party, Sinn Fein ("We ourselves"), wants Ireland to break away from the United Kingdom. Sinn Fein's fighting force, the Irish Republican Army (IRA), is attacking pro-British Irish people and damaging government property. British ex-servicemen have been sent to Ireland to help the regular troops. They are known as the "Black and Tans" because of the color of their uniforms. They themselves are becoming as violent as the IRA. There is now a civil war in Ireland.

Black and Tans search a Sinn Feiner.

WOMEN HELP ELECT HARDING

Nov. 2, Washington Warren Harding is our new President. This was the first election in which women were allowed to vote for a President. American women have been fighting for this right in a struggle that began about 50 years ago. The 19th Amendment to the United States Constitution, ratified in August of this year, guarantees them full voting privileges. The amendment says, "The right of citizens of the United States to vote shall not be denied or abridged by the United States or by any state on account of sex."

Women have had the vote within some states for years. The United States Territory of Wyoming, where women have been voting since 1869, was the first to grant this right. By the beginning of this year, 15 states had adopted woman suffrage. Now Warren Harding, our 27th President, has been elected with the help of women's votes.

Women cast their votes for the first time.

THE BOLSHEVIKS WIN RUSSIA'S CIVIL WAR

Nov. 20, Petrograd The Bolsheviks (Communists) formed a government in Russia three years ago, but thousands of Russians have been fighting against them. Now, after a fierce battle, their White Army has been defeated by the Bolshevik Red Army. All Russians are now forced to accept Lenin's Communist government.

NEWS IN BRIEF . . .

BOMB KILLS 30

Sept. 16, New York At noon today at Broad and Wall streets an explosion killed 30 and injured 300. Windows were shattered for blocks around. The entire financial district was in a state of panic. The police believe the blast was caused by a time bomb placed in a one-horse truck right in front of the J.P. Morgan Building by Reds or anarchists.

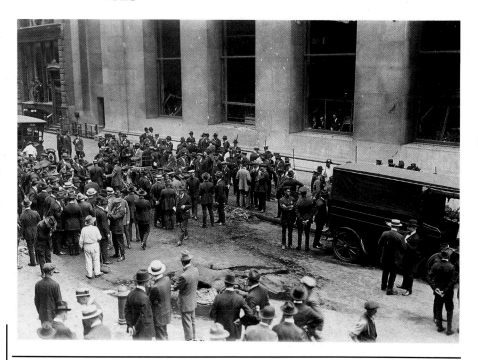

BASEBALL SCANDAL

Sept. 28, Chicago Eight Chicago White Sox players were indicted today for conspiring with gamblers to "fix" the 1919 World Series. "Shoeless" Joe Jackson was among those indicted. If convicted, the players face up to five years in prison. A young fan recently met Jackson outside the courtroom and cried, "Say it ain't so, Joe."

AMERICANS EXCEL AT OLYMPIC GAMES

Sept. 12, Antwerp, Belgium The seventh Olympic Games ended today in Belgium. This is the first time the games have been held since the war. In all, 29 nations took part. A 13-year-old American girl, Aileen Riggen, won the springboard diving competition. Her gold medal was one of 41 won by the United States — a remarkable achievement. The first ice hockey matches to be played at the Olympics were greatly enjoyed by spectators. The ice hockey competition was won by a team from Canada.

FASHIONS INFLUENCED BY THE WAR

Nov. 11, Paris This is the second anniversary of the ending of the Great War. During the war, from 1914 to 1918, hundreds of women worked to help the war effort. They had to wear clothes that were shorter and more practical. Today's fashions for women are comfortable and casual. The waistline drops to the hip, and skirt hems fall just above the ankle. Fashionable ladies have had their long hair cut short and waved.

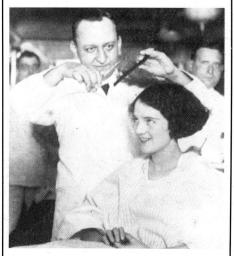
Smart young women are having their hair "bobbed."

WILSON WINS PEACE PRIZE

Dec. 10, Washington Former President Wilson was tonight awarded the Nobel Peace Prize in Christiana, Norway. The award recognized his work in restoring peace to Europe after the Great War. Whether Wilson can enjoy this honor is a question. He suffered a stroke in September 1919, which left him partially paralyzed. Also, the Senate voted to bar the U.S. from joining the new League of Nations, the cornerstone of Wilson's peace plan. In addition, the country rejected Wilson's policies by electing Republican Warren G. Harding President.

HOW LONG DO WE LIVE?

Dec., Washington A recent survey published here shows that an average American man lives a little over 53 years. An American woman lives one year longer. Life expectancy has gone up remarkably in recent years. Twenty years ago a man might expect to live only until he was 49.

1921

SACCO AND VANZETTI CONVICTED OF MURDER

July 14, Dedham, Mass. After deliberating for almost eight hours, the jury found Nicola Sacco and Bartolomeo Vanzetti guilty of killing the guard of a shoe factory in South Braintree, Massachusetts, during a payroll robbery. The trial has had wide attention. Many American liberals and members of labor groups believe that the two Italian immigrants were convicted because of their anarchist political beliefs and not because of any evidence presented at the trial. (Anarchists support the overthrow of all governments.)

Both Sacco, a shoemaker, and Vanzetti, a fish peddler, denied having any part in the murder. Police have so far not been able to trace any of the $16,000 stolen to either of these men.

GERMAN MARKS ARE ALMOST WORTHLESS

Nov. 7, Germany Britain and France have sent Germany a bill for $50 billion. They need these "reparations" to pay their own war debts and to rebuild France and Belgium. The French have occupied the Ruhr, Germany's industrial center. They will take coal away as their share of the reparations. Germany's financial crisis has made its currency very weak. Seven years ago a $5 bill was worth 20 marks. Today you would need 1,200 marks in exchange for $5. The government has resigned. A small political party, the National Socialists (Nazis), blames Jews and capitalists. The leader of the party is Herr Adolf Hitler.

German children play with bundles of money. German currency is virtually wastepaper.

AMERICA'S UNKNOWN SOLDIER BURIED

Nov. 11, Washington America's Unknown Soldier was buried today, Armistice Day, three years after the end of the war. The tomb is in Arlington National Cemetery in Virginia. The body has been lying in state in the rotunda of the Capitol for several days. Thousands of people have come to walk slowly past the flag-covered coffin to pay their respects to an unknown American hero.

RUSSIANS ARE DYING OF HUNGER

Aug. 4, St. Petersburg As is true worldwide, there is mass unemployment in Russia. The civil war interfered with farming and the economy suffered. The harvest failed, following a long drought. Many villages are reporting epidemics of the diseases cholera and typhoid. Up to 20,000 people face starvation. Lenin has asked other countries for help for the starving.

THE LEAGUE OF NATIONS SOLVES TWO DISPUTES

Sept. 22, Geneva Three Balkan countries, Latvia, Lithuania, and Estonia, have joined the League of Nations. The League of Nations has already settled two international problems. Last year Sweden and Finland disagreed about possession of a small island. This year the League settled a frontier dispute between Turkey and Iraq (formerly Mesopotamia). These were minor problems, but the results are encouraging for the League's future.

Michael Collins, head of the Irish Free State.

American Businesses Face a Recession

September 26 Nearly four million people are unemployed in America. The government is going to create jobs for as many as possible. Immigration has been restricted. The country cannot afford to take in any more unemployed foreigners.

WOMEN EARN LESS THAN MEN

July 19, Oakland, Calif. Dr. Amelia Reinhardt, president of Mills College, told the delegates of the National Federation of Business and Professional Women's Clubs that eight million women are employed. Most are teachers or secretaries. Almost two out of eight are married. On every level, women earn less than men. Many professions, especially medicine, effectively bar women.

NAVAL TREATY ENDS WARSHIP BUILDING

Dec. 14, Washington By a treaty signed yesterday, the United States, Britain, France, and Japan agreed to limit the number of warships each may have. This means that Britain will no longer have the largest fleet of ships in the world. Over 650 British ships will have to be scrapped. Many dockworkers and shipbuilders will lose their jobs.

IRELAND IS DIVIDED

Dec. 6, Downing Street, London Today British ministers signed a treaty with members of Sinn Fein which made southern Ireland independent of the United Kingdom. There are 32 counties in Ireland; 26 have joined together as the Irish Free State. The other six, to be called Northern Ireland, will remain part of the United Kingdom. The British government hopes that this will end the bitter fighting in Ireland. But Mr. Michael Collins, who signed the treaty for Ireland, knows that many southerners want the whole of Ireland to be independent. "I have signed my death warrant," he said. Nobody knows how seriously he meant this. He certainly has many enemies.

NEWS IN BRIEF . . .

DIABETES SUFFERERS CAN HOPE FOR RELIEF

July 30, Toronto, Canada Two doctors, Frederick Banting and Charles Best, have discovered that people who have diabetes can be helped by injections of insulin. With this treatment, sufferers may hope to live longer. At present, if you are diagnosed as diabetic, you will probably live for less than five more years.

DANCES AND CLOTHES CENSORED

May 15, Richmond, Va. Many people consider new styles of dress and dance proof of a serious moral problem. Virginia lawmakers are deciding how low dress and blouse necklines may be. Utah legislators are discussing a law to jail women who wear skirts more than three inches above the ankle. New York has already passed a law giving the state the right to censor dances.

Best, Banting, and the first dog successfully treated with insulin.

CARUSO IS DEAD

Aug. 3, New York Enrico Caruso, the leading Italian tenor, has died at the age of 48. He was born in Naples. In his twenties he sang in operas at the famous La Scala Opera House in Milan. For the last 18 years he has been the principal tenor at New York's Metropolitan Opera House.

LITTLE MISS AMERICA IS CROWNED

Sept. 7, Atlantic City A blonde, blue-eyed girl of 16 has become the first "Miss America." Eight girls entered the contest. Already dozens are preparing for the next one. The city's businessmen believe a yearly competition will be good for the tourist trade.

Miss Margaret Gorman, the first Miss America.

TULSA RACE RIOT

June 1, Tulsa, Okla. A series of events yesterday has left 85 dead, hundreds injured, and thousands of Negroes homeless because of fires. A Negro bootblack was charged with attacking a white woman. When rumors spread that the Negro would be lynched, 500 heavily armed Negroes gathered near the courthouse where the bootblack was held. Police surrounded the building, and the Negroes fired.

Whites broke into sporting goods stores to steal weapons. Then they invaded the city's Negro section.

Negroes being escorted into building under armed guard.

1922

IRELAND

RESENTMENT AGAINST ANGLO-IRISH TREATY

May 31, Dublin Mr. Michael Collins, head of the Irish Free State government, has a grave problem. The "republicans," those who do not want a separate Irish Free State, are in revolt. They have murdered soldiers, and in April seized the courthouse. Some of the republicans were Mr. Collins's most trusted men. Many Irishmen who served in the British Army have joined the army of the Free State. The republicans say this is the same army with a new name. They are bitter because Mr. Collins is using the army against them. They think he has betrayed southern Ireland.

COLLINS GUNNED DOWN IN CORK

Aug. 22, Cork In June Mr. Collins sent Free State troops to force the republicans out of Dublin's courthouse. He also sent troops to besiege republicans in the city of Cork. These acts made him "the most hated man in the Irish government." Now Mr. Collins has been shot dead in an ambush. He came to this city where he was born, two days ago. He said to friends, "They won't shoot me in my own country."

THE FREE STATE STANDS ALONE

Dec. 17, Dublin British troops have left the Irish Free State, which now has no ties with Britain.

FAMOUS REPORTER DIES

Jan. 27, New York Newspaper reporter Nellie Bly died of pneumonia today. She was 54. She is well known for a report of her trip around the world. She finished her journey in less time than the storybook character Phileas Fogg's amazing 80 days. Her exposé of cruelty in a mental hospital spurred reforms nationwide.

A NEW GOVERNMENT IN ITALY

THE FASCIST LEADER PERMITS ILLEGAL ACTS

Jan. 30, Milan Italy's government is weak and its economy poor. The Communists want a Russian-type government. Many others are joining Benito Mussolini's Fascists in Milan. The Fascists are known to physically attack Communists, many of whom have been beaten up. There are 35 Fascists in Italy's parliament, the Chamber of Deputies.

"BLACKSHIRTS" SEIZE POWER

Aug. 3, Milan Dressed in their uniform of brown trousers and black shirts, the Fascists under Benito Mussolini marched into Milan's industrial area and stopped a general strike. They terrorized the workers and burned trade union buildings. Police and troops were unable to stop them.

FASCIST LEADER IS NEW PRIME MINISTER

Nov. 25, Rome Last month 24,000 Fascists marched into Rome from Milan. The king of Italy was afraid of their strength. He asked Benito Mussolini to lead the government. Mussolini has now become the dictator of Italy. He has told the Chamber of Deputies that all members must obey him. They have meekly agreed.

Mussolini (second from right) with fellow Fascists.

INDIAN NATIONALIST JAILED

March 18, Ahmedabad, Gujarat Mohandas Gandhi's policy of noncooperation with the British has led to civil disobedience. People are refusing to pay their taxes. A British magistrate sentenced Mr. Gandhi to six years' imprisonment for encouraging people to break the law. The magistrate said he realized that to millions of people Mr. Gandhi was "a great patriot and a great leader."

THE NEW POPE APPEALS FOR PEACE

Feb. 6, Rome Cardinal Achille Ratti has been elected pope, just three weeks after the previous pope died. He has chosen the name Pius XI. After the election the pope went out onto the balcony of St. Peter's and blessed the crowd. He prayed for "that peace for which the world sighs so much."

PHARAOH'S TOMB IS OPENED

Nov. 30, Thebes, Egypt There was great excitement yesterday in a desert valley here. Dr. Howard Carter has discovered the tomb of Pharaoh Tutankhamun, who lived 3,000 years ago. Dr. Carter tells us what happened as he opened the royal tomb:

"At first I could see nothing, the hot air escaping from the chamber causing the candle to flicker. But presently, as my eyes grew accustomed to the light, details of the room emerged slowly from the mist, strange animals, statues, and gold — everywhere the glint of gold. For a moment — an eternity it must have seemed to the others standing by, I was struck dumb; then Lord Carnarvon inquired anxiously—'Can you see anything?'"

'Yes,' I replied, . . . 'wonderful things. . .'"

EGYPT NOW HAS A KING

March 16, Cairo The people of Egypt are jubilant because the British protectorate over Egypt has ended after 40 years. The sultan of Egypt has become King Fuad I. Coins will be struck in his name, and stamps will bear his portrait.

KEMAL'S VICTORY THREATENS STRAITS

Oct. 30, Turkey Since 1920, when the Greeks were given much of Turkey's territory, the Turkish army has been fighting to regain the land. This army, led by Mustafa Kemal, has reached the Dardanelles. The Turks want to control these important straits, which are a neutral zone.

(The Tomb of Tutankhamun, Vol. 1, Howard Carter and A.C. Mace, Cassell pic, 1923)

NEWS IN BRIEF . . .

THE MEDIEVAL LOOK IS MODERN

April 30, Paris This year, evening clothes have low waistlines, wide sleeves, and trailing hems. Long bead necklaces complete the ensemble. The fashion designers say that they are influenced by medieval clothing. What is not medieval is the new bust bodice. It flattens the bosom to give a boyish line. The flatter you are, the better!

"Flappers" — the new slang word for fashionable young women — wear their hair bobbed, with a hair band worn over the forehead.

NEW MAGAZINE PUBLISHED

Feb. 5, New York DeWitt Wallace and his wife, Lila Acheson, published Vol. 1, No. 1 of the *Reader's Digest* today. The pocket-sized magazine has already sold 1,500 copies. Wallace, of St. Paul, Minnesota, got the idea for the magazine from his great interest in magazine articles and his natural ability to condense them. The publishers say their aim is to entertain and to inspire people to live better lives.

ANNIE OAKLEY BREAKS RECORD

March 5, North Carolina Famous sharpshooter Annie Oakley started shooting at the age of nine. For years she was a star of Buffalo Bill's Wild West Show. Today she broke all records for women's trap shooting. Miss Oakley hit 98 out of 100 clay targets thrown.

The beautiful Lillian Russell in one of her elaborate outfits.

LILLIAN RUSSELL DIES

June 6, New York Famous singer and actress Lillian Russell died today at 61. She began her career in light opera. Miss Russell was known for her gorgeous jewelry and her costumes, particularly her hats. In the late 1800s, she was considered the ideal beauty.

ULYSSES BANNED AND BURNED

March 5, New York On Mr. James Joyce's fortieth birthday, which was February 2, his new novel, *Ulysses*, was published in Paris. Today a newspaper reviewer called it a work of genius, but did not like its vulgarity. Mr. Joyce uses some words that are not generally seen in print. The book is banned in the United States. When someone tried to mail copies to New York, the post office seized and burned them. Some European travelers have succeeeded in smuggling copies past the customs officers.

1923

CHAOS IN GERMANY

WORKERS ARE RIOTING IN THE RUHR

Jan. 25, Weimar There was trouble in the Ruhr this month. The German chancellor told factory workers and miners to obey rules and work. But many refused to work at all, and went on strike. They abused French troops as they loaded coal onto trucks to take to France. Fighting broke out, and the French arrested many of the workers.

THE FRENCH MAKE THE CRISIS WORSE

Feb. 1, Weimar The French are preventing coal from reaching German factories and homes. There is less and less to buy in the shops. Food is very expensive. A five-dollar bill is now worth 220,000 marks. The Bavarians of southeast Germany have set up a dictatorship of their own. They have no faith in the German government.

CARTER IN TUTANKHAMUN'S CHAMBER

Feb. 20, Cairo It has taken Dr. Howard Carter many months to clear the first room of Tutankhamun's tomb. Three days ago he carefully removed the wall that seals the burial chamber. There he found, and opened, an enormous gold shrine. Inside there were three more shrines, each smaller than the last. The fourth contained a stone coffin decorated at each corner with a winged goddess. It may contain the pharaoh's body.

TEAPOT DOME SCANDAL GROWS

Oct. 25, Washington Last year government oil reserves at Elk Hills and Teapot Dome were leased to private oil companies by then Secretary of the Interior Albert B. Fall. Mr. Fall failed to get competitive bids from other companies. He said he could get a better price this way. However, it appears that he made personal profits from these transactions.

Copyright, New York Tribune

"THE FIRST GOOD LAUGH THEY'VE HAD IN YEARS"

DISCOVERER OF X RAYS DIES

Feb. 10, Germany Dr. Wilhelm Röntgen, who won the Nobel Prize in 1901 for discovering X rays, died yesterday. X rays are used to show the bones and internal organs of the body. They help doctors to diagnose disease, and surgeons to perform operations. Röntgen refused to make any money from his discovery, and he died penniless.

HARVARD BANS DISCRIMINATION

April 9, Cambridge, Mass. The overseers of Harvard University voted unanimously to maintain Harvard's "traditional policy of freedom from discrimination on grounds of race or religion." Discrimination against Negroes became a public issue when the president of the university wrote to a graduate that his Negro son could not live in a freshman dormitory.

RUSSIA HAS A NEW NAME

July 6, Moscow Russia is to be called the Union of Soviet Socialist Republics (USSR). The country is a collection of different republican councils ("soviets") under one central government. It contains about 100 different nationalities. Lenin, the Bolshevik leader, is trying to mold them all into one nation, led by the Communist party.

ILLEGAL SOCIETY USES VIOLENCE

Sept. 15, Oklahoma A society known as the Ku Klux Klan (KKK) is causing racial hatred here. Klan members dress in white robes. Pointed hoods leave only their eyes showing. They terrorize Indians, Negroes, Jews, and Catholics, whom they call "un-American." Oklahoma's governor has formed a national guard to stop this violent behavior, but in other southern states the KKK continues its terrorism unchecked.

Klansmen may look absurd, but they are killers.

TERRIBLE EARTHQUAKE IN JAPAN

Sept. 3, Tokyo News is coming through of a severe earthquake in Tokyo. It happened two days ago, when workers were going home to lunch. In some areas the ground rose up by 10 feet (3 m). Japanese houses are made of wood and paper. Many caught fire when the earthquake overturned lamps and cooking stoves. Other fires were started by broken electric cables and gas lines. Altogether about 100,000 people have died, and 2½ million are homeless. Half the city is completely destroyed.

The Japanese city of Yokohama devastated by the earthquake. A terrible fire followed.

PRESIDENT DIES, VICE-PRESIDENT SWORN IN

Aug. 3, Washington Mr. Calvin Coolidge, the Vice-President, was today sworn in as the new President of the United States. The former President, Mr. Warren Harding, died of a stroke on his return home from a hectic business trip.

President Coolidge agrees with the U.S. policy not to join the League of Nations. He has been elected as the economy is beginning to improve. Americans feel that better times are on the way.

THE TURKS WIN THE DARDANELLES

July 24, Turkey Mustafa Kemal and his Turkish army have won the battle for the Dardanelles. The British have agreed to leave the former neutral zone. A million Greeks are now living in Turkish territory. There are almost as many Turks in Greece. The League of Nations is going to try to exchange the two "foreign" populations.

Mustafa Kemal (left), the victorious Turkish general.

THE MARK TOPPLES STILL FURTHER

Sept. 12, Weimar A five-dollar bill is now equal to a staggering 600,000,000 marks. You need a suitcase full of money when you go shopping. Germany has a new chancellor, Dr. Gustav Stresemann. He has ordered strikers in the Ruhr to return to work. He believes that cooperation with the rest of Europe is a better policy than resistance.

At a rally in Nuremberg this week Adolf Hitler strongly criticized the government.

A new German banknote for 20 billion marks.

BANKS WILL BUY YOUR MONEY

Nov. 15, Weimar The German government is asking people to return their paper money to the bank. In exchange, everyone will get new coins and notes. The Allies are going to reconsider the way in which reparations should be paid.

HITLER IS IN JAIL

Nov. 12, Munich Four days ago Adolf Hitler, with a group of Nazis, burst into a beer hall where a Bavarian official was making a speech. He fired a shot into the air. "The revolution has begun," he shouted. He then led the Nazis towards the town square, but they were stopped by police. Many were arrested. Hitler is now in jail. Another Nazi, Hermann Goering, was badly wounded and is in the hospital. The Bavarians refused to support this attempt at a national revolution.

NEWS IN BRIEF . . .

ANTI-LYNCHING CAMPAIGN

April 28, Missouri Representative Leonidas C. Dyer of Missouri will make a tour of the West. He will speak on behalf of his proposed anti-lynching bill. The National Association for the Advancement of Colored People is paying for his trip. The bill would affect state officers and mob members accused of being involved in a lynching. They would have to be tried in federal courts if state courts refused to act in the matter.

The majority of Southerners and Democrats are against the bill. They say the proposed legislation is unconstitutional.

RIN-TIN-TIN IS FAMOUS

Dec., Hollywood During the Great War (1914–1918), an American soldier found a starving German shepherd dog in the trenches in France. He adopted it and later brought it home. The dog, Rin-Tin-Tin, is now working in movies. He is such a popular star that he has his own fan mail. His latest movie is *The Night Cry*.

Rin-Tin-Tin goes to the rescue in *Tracked by the Police*.

PILOTS FLY NONSTOP TO COAST

May 3, San Diego, Calif. Army pilots Oakley Kelley and John Macready completed the first nonstop coast-to-coast flight today. They left from Roosevelt Field, Long Island, and landed in San Diego about 27 hours later. They covered 2,600 miles, at an average speed of 100 miles an hour.

Their flight shows that it may soon be possible for commercial airlines to provide coast-to-coast service on a regular basis.

DANCING FOR PROFIT IS NO FUN

April 14, Los Angeles The dance marathon is the new craze in America. The record for nonstop dancing is 90 hours. This strenuous exercise is a danger to health. Couples have been taken to the hospital after collapsing on the dance floor. After he had danced for 86 hours one young man fell down dead. Why do they do it? There is a big cash prize for the record-breaker.

A girl collapses in exhaustion at a dance marathon.

1924

ATROCITY IN ITALY
FASCISTS WIN THE ELECTIONS

April 17, Rome The Fascists have won the general election by a huge majority. Benito Mussolini and his party are back in power. The Communist candidates were defeated. Italians hope that the Fascists will bring in much-needed reforms.

MUSSOLINI'S CRITIC IS KIDNAPPED

June 10, Rome In May, Socialist landowner Giacomo Matteotti accused the Fascists of rigging the election. He said they used threats and cheated. He is an outspoken critic of the Fascists. Now Signor Matteotti has disappeared. Passersby on a busy street in Rome watched horrified as he was bundled into a car. The car drove off at high speed. The Fascists are suspected of plotting the boldfaced kidnapping.

MISSING LANDOWNER FOUND DEAD

Aug. 17, Rome Signor Matteotti's body was found yesterday in a shallow grave a few miles from Rome. He had been beaten to death. The people of Rome have laid flowers on the pavement where he was kidnapped. His widow is sure that the Fascists are responsible. She has appealed to Benito Mussolini to return her husband's body, but the Fascist leader denies all knowledge of the killing. There are no clues as to who murdered him.

LEOPOLD AND LOEB CONFESS

May 31, Chicago Nathan Leopold, 19, and Richard Loeb, 18, are sons of wealthy families. They have confessed to murdering a 14-year-old boy. They gave Bobby Franks, a distant cousin of Loeb's, a ride. Then they beat him to death and hid his body. They said they wanted to see if they could commit the perfect crime. Their lawyer is the famous Clarence Darrow. He plans to offer a new kind of defense — mental illness.

NOVEL SHOWS INDIAN DILEMMA

Feb. 4, London Mr. E.M. Forster's new novel *A Passage to India* is about relationships between Indians and the British. Empire-builders think there should be no social contact between the two. Mr. Forster shows the misery that such attitudes, and such relationships, bring. The book may make some Europeans more sympathetic to Gandhi's views. The Indian leader was freed today after serving two years of his six-year sentence.

COMRADE V. LENIN DIES

Jan. 21, Moscow Vladimir Lenin is dead. Seven years ago he led the successful revolution that brought Russia's Communist government to power. Not all his reforms were successful. He made peasants sell their produce to the state at low fixed prices. They began to grow less and less food. He tried to correct this mistake, but the last seven years have not been easy for rural Russians. Lenin's body will be embalmed and laid in a mausoleum in Red Square. In his honor, Petrograd will be renamed Leningrad.

Joseph Stalin (his name means "man of steel") may be the future leader of the USSR. For the time being he will be one of a council of three people in power, but he is known as an ambitious man.

MAJOR MOVIE MERGER

April 17, Hollywood A new motion picture company was formed yesterday when Marcus Loew finalized the merger of Metro Pictures, Goldwyn Pictures, and the Louis B. Mayer Company. The total worth of the combined companies is $65 million, making this one of the largest mergers in the history of the movie industry.

The name of the enormous new company will be the Metro-Goldwyn-Mayer Corporation. The trademark for MGM will be a roaring lion.

FINN IS TIRELESS IN OLYMPIC GAMES

July 27, Paris The hero of this year's Olympic Games is Finnish runner Paavo Nurmi. He won six gold medals. He set two Olympic records: he ran the 1,500 meters in 3 minutes 53.6 seconds, and the 5,000 meters in 14 minutes 31.2 seconds. He had only one hour's rest between the two events. Many other runners have collapsed from heat exhaustion. Harold Abrahams of Great Britain won the 100 meters, equaling the Olympic record. Johnny Weissmuller of the United States won five gold medals for swimming.

The Finnish runner Paavo Nurmi streaks away ahead of the competition.

NEW YORK WELCOMES WILL ROGERS HOME

June 30, New York Theatergoers were thrilled to welcome Will Rogers back to the New York stage last night in the new Ziegfeld Follies production. He kept the audience laughing as he spun his familiar lasso and told brand-new jokes. However, he said, "I don't make jokes—I just watch the government and report the facts." America's "cowboy philosopher" was in top form.

TILDEN IS NATIONAL TENNIS CHAMP AGAIN

Sept. 2, Forest Hills, N.Y. When "Big Bill" Tilden beat William Johnston here today he became national tennis champion for the fifth straight year. Tilden sailed easily through the match, besting his opponent 6–1, 9–7, 4–2. Spectators said that in the first set he played some of the greatest tennis ever seen here or elsewhere.

William Tatem Tilden, Jr. was born in Philadelphia. He was the first American to win at Wimbledon (1920 and 1921).

COOLIDGE ELECTED PRESIDENT

Nov. 4, Washington Calvin Coolidge has been elected to a full term as President of the United States. He has been serving in that office since the death of President Warren G. Harding in August of last year. Coolidge, a Republican, had no close competitors for his party's nomination. The shy, quiet New Englander is popular because he seems to represent the old-fashioned virtues of the American pioneers. Coolidge's campaign slogan was "Keep Cool with Coolidge."

NEWS IN BRIEF . . .

BLACK ACTOR IS THREATENED

May 15, New York Mr. Paul Bustill Robeson, the American Negro singer, has been rehearsing for tonight's opening of *All God's Chillun Got Wings*. He plays a Negro man married to a white woman. The KKK says this is immoral. The star has already received hundreds of threatening letters. One letter said a bomb was going to be planted in the theater tonight. The police searched, but found nothing.

HOSPITAL IN HEART OF AFRICA

April 30, West Africa Dr. Albert Schweitzer returned on Easter Saturday to Lambaréné, 125 miles (200 km) up the Ogowe River in West Africa. By Easter Monday he was seeing patients. He is now rebuilding the hospital he started in 1913 for African villagers. Before he studied medicine, Dr. Schweitzer was a distinguished organist, and principal of a religious college. He is the author of books on Bach, and on Jesus' teaching. His hospital is always crowded.

FIRST WOMAN GOVERNOR

Nov. 4, Austin, Texas Miriam "Ma" Ferguson became the first woman to be elected a U.S. governor. Mrs. Ferguson said she ran to vindicate her husband, who was impeached as governor in 1917. He was accused of using state money for personal purposes. Mrs. Ferguson is an outspoken opponent of the Ku Klux Klan.

FIRST LONG-DISTANCE CALL

June 2, Vancluse, Australia Australia spoke to England last night—by wireless. It is the first time a wireless (rather than telegraph) has been used over such a great distance. The radio pioneer Guglielmo Marconi said that one day there will be telephones all over the world. The calls were between Poldhu in Cornwall, England, and Vancluse near Sydney, in Australia.

THE ORIENTAL LOOK

Autumn, Paris, France This year's fashions have a very graceful, Japanese feel. Typical of the style are Worth's evening dresses.

1925

THE AMERICAN DREAM WORLD

AMERICAN BUSINESS BOOMS

Jan. 31, New York In our country, "business" has become the most important thing in many people's lives. It is exciting to be able to earn enough for luxuries like cars, washing machines, and radios. For entertainment people visit movie theaters, nightclubs, and vaudeville theaters. Their parents had none of these things.

WHO WOULD WALK IF HE COULD RIDE?

June 30, Detroit Cars have been the talk of this town ever since Mr. Henry Ford set up his factory. His black "Tin Lizzies" are cheap and reliable. Now the Chrysler Company is trying to persuade rich business people that a six-cylinder *de luxe* car would suit their style better. The car is a symbol of success. Real estate agents say that when people buy houses, the garage is as important as the house itself. Everyone wants a big new car.

A PLACE IN THE SUN

Aug. 31, Florida There is a housing and land boom in this sunny state. The plots of land are not cheap, but there seem to be plenty of buyers. The houses they build are in all styles: Spanish, Dutch, colonial American. Many of them have swimming pools. This luxurious way of life is envied by many and condemned by some critics.

IS CHARLES DARWIN RIGHT?

July 21, Tennessee The state of Tennessee has a new law which says that Charles Darwin's theory of evolution may not be taught in schools. The theory says life began with very simple creatures, and all present animals, including humans, evolved over millions of years. Our ancestors, Darwin said, were like apes. Today, Mr. John Scopes has been found guilty of teaching the theory of evolution. The prosecution lawyer, Mr. William Bryan, believes in the Bible creation story of Adam and Eve. Though Mr. Scopes' lawyer, Mr. Clarence Darrow, showed that Mr. Bryan knew nothing about history and modern science, he lost the case. The teacher had clearly broken the law, and he was fined $100. However, Mr. Darrow criticized the new law, saying that ignorant people should not control children's education.

FITZGERALD PUBLISHES NEW NOVEL

Dec., New York This year saw the publication of F. Scott Fitzgerald's novel *The Great Gatsby*. Fitzgerald has been popular since the publication of his collection of short stories called *Tales of the Jazz Age*. Although *The Great Gatsby* has not been as popular as Fitzgerald's earlier works, some critics feel it has the makings of a classic. The novel exposes the false glamour, awful boredom, and moral emptiness of the nation's very rich. Fitzgerald himself also takes part in this pleasure-seeking way of life. However, instead of seeing it as the "American dream" come true, he condemns it as basically artificial and sooner or later unsatisfying.

"OUR PRODUCT IS THE BEST"

Oct. 30, New York When you have something to sell, it pays to advertise. In America 600,000 people are creating a dream world in which we can all have shining teeth, clear complexions, and "whiter than white" clothes. We are constantly urged to buy, buy, buy. Even President Coolidge was advertised with the slogan "Keep Cool with Coolidge."

PLAYWRIGHT GIVEN TOP HONOR

Dec. 10, London Mr. George Bernard Shaw has been awarded the Nobel Prize for Literature, after the success of his play *St. Joan*. It is based on old documents written in France when the French girl Joan of Arc was burned at the stake by the English nearly 500 years ago. Mr. Shaw, who was born in Dublin, began his career as a journalist. His previous plays include *Man and Superman* (1903) and *Pygmalion* (1912).

A scene from the first stage production of *St. Joan* in London. Joan of Arc, dressed as a soldier, rallies her followers against the English enemy, who were trying to conquer France.

MUSSOLINI DICTATES TO ITALY

Nov. 20, Rome Under Benito Mussolini's government malaria has been wiped out in the south; the trains are punctual; and nobody goes on strike. But in spite of these advantages, many Italians are not happy. They do not like being told what to do and what to say. Mussolini has banned all left-wing (Socialist and Communist) parties. Cabinet ministers who do not agree with fascism have resigned. The newspapers have to print government propaganda.

HITLER PUBLISHES A BOOK

July 18, Germany Adolf Hitler wrote *Mein Kampf* (My Struggle) while he was in prison. His book, published today, is a mixture of autobiography, politics, and arguments against the Jews. In the book he also says that people of one nationality should live under one rule. There are millions of Germans in Russia, Poland, Czechoslovakia, and Austria. Politicians all over Europe are afraid that if he ever came to power, Hitler might try to invade these countries.

NEWS IN BRIEF . . .

SOLAR ECLIPSE

Jan. 5, New York A complete solar eclipse took place here yesterday at 9:11 A.M. The amazing sight was observed from land, sea, and air. Scientists photographed the display from a dirigible. The mayor watched from the steps of City Hall. Thousands gazed at the brilliant show from positions at Battery Park.

DUKE IS RICHEST UNIVERSITY

Oct. 27, North Carolina The "tobacco king" and philanthropist James Buchanan Duke died last night. His will made Duke University in Durham, North Carolina, the richest in the country. Last year he set up a trust fund of $40 million for the school. Under his will, that gift doubles.

Duke, the founder of the American Tobacco Company, was born poor. He began his career hauling tobacco with "a pair of blind mules."

THE TRAMP IS BACK

Aug. 6, Los Angeles Charlie Chaplin's new movie is called *The Gold Rush*. It features the famous little tramp with mustache and cane. He is still dressed in a derby that is too small for him and baggy trousers.

CHARLESTON SETS THE FASHION

Autumn, Paris Large collars and floppy bows are this year's fashion tip. The daring are wearing their skirts above the knee, showing pink flesh-colored silk or rayon stockings. This is just the thing for dancing the Charleston, the newest dance craze. It seems that everyone in the U.S. has already learned the steps. Americans have been doing the Charleston to the music of popular jazz bands for some time. Now Europeans are kicking up their heels, twisting their knees, and turning in their toes in the "dance of the decade."

THE PHARAOH TUTANKHAMUN WAS ONLY EIGHTEEN

Nov. 13, Egypt Dr. Howard Carter has uncovered the mummified body of Tutankhamun. The mummy was covered with gold, and on the pharaoh's face was a wonderful gold and blue mask. Nearly 10 jewels were scattered over his body. It is not surprising that in ancient times, jewel and treasure thieves broke into royal graves. Here at last is one which they failed to rob. Scientists say that the pharaoh was only about 18 years old when he died.

The golden mask of Pharaoh Tutankhamun, from about 1340 B.C.

POLICE RAID GANGSTERS' HIDEOUT

Dec. 3, New York The police have raided a warehouse where gangsters were storing alcohol. It is the biggest haul since Prohibition began. But people are still hiding "bootleg" (illegal) whiskey or gin in unusual places: hot-water bottles, shoe heels, perfume bottles, Russian boots. Bootleg liquor is not hard to make — it is just raw alcohol with color and flavoring added. Even if it doesn't taste like the real thing, everyone wants to buy it. Real whiskey can still be had on prescription for a variety of ailments — including "thirstitis." Doctors are very popular!

1926

BRITAIN'S FIRST GENERAL STRIKE

May 10, London For the first time in British history all union members are out on strike. The strike started when miners put their tools down and picketed the mines. Their pay had been cut and their hours increased. Now, in support of the miners, thousands of workers have gone on strike all over England. Transportation workers stayed home and college students are driving the buses and trains. Electricity and water services are still working normally, but newspapers are on strike. Food supplies are being collected in Hyde Park in London and distributed all over the country by soldiers in armored cars.

FIRST WOMAN SWIMS CHANNEL

Aug. 6, New York This city was deeply stirred today when news came that 19-year-old Gertrude Ederle, a New Yorker, had become the first woman to swim the English Channel. Miss Ederle was faster than any of the men who have gone before her, completing the crossing in 14 hours, 31 minutes. Sebastian Tirabocchi, an Italian swimmer, established the best previous time in 1923 — 16 hours, 23 minutes. Miss Ederle said during the swim, "I'm doing it for mummy." Her mother had sent a series of cables urging her to keep swimming. Her father and sister accompanied Miss Ederle in a boat throughout her swim.

Demonstrating strikers clash with police in the street.

FLORIDA HURRICANE KILLS 1,000

Sept. 19, Jacksonville A powerful hurricane banged into a 60-mile stretch of Florida's lower east coast yesterday. It is believed that 1,000 people have died in the storm and another 3,000 have been injured. Many towns were destroyed or flooded. All ships in Miami's harbor were sunk. At least 38,000 people have been left homeless. The damages may reach $100,000,000. Miami is hardest hit.

AFRICA IS THE "CRADLE OF MANKIND"

Jan., Kimberley, South Africa Mr. Raymond Dart, who studies our very early history, says that Africa is "the cradle of mankind." Two years ago, on November 28, 1924, he found the skull of a child. He found it at Tuang near Kimberley. Mr. Dart thinks the skull belonged to an apelike creature that lived about 5 million years ago. The skull is more like a human's than an ape's. Mr. Dart says that modern men and women evolved from these creatures. He has given the species the Latin name *Australopithecus*, which means "Southern Man." Mr. Dart is only 33 and many of his critics will not take his discoveries seriously.

A NEW KINGDOM IS BORN IN ARABIA

Jan. 9, Mecca, Arabia Abd al-Aziz ibn Sa'ud is one of the most powerful Arab leaders of this century. He left Kuwait, where his family had been exiled, 25 years ago. Now he has become ruler of most of Arabia. Yesterday in the holy city of Mecca he was crowned King of Najd and the Hejaz. He has called his kingdom Saudi Arabia, after the Sa'ud name.

AMERICANS SWEEP BRITISH OPEN

June 25, Atlanta, Georgia Americans are celebrating because the first four places in the British Open golf championship have been won by U.S. citizens. For the first time in 29 years the top winner was an amateur. He is Bobby Jones, an ex-lawyer from this city. When he dropped his final putt, 5,000 spectators cheered.

AFRICANS BARRED FROM WELL-PAID JOBS

Nov. 20, Pretoria, South Africa South Africa, along with Canada, New Zealand, and Australia, has become a self-governing dominion. This will make no difference to the majority of South Africans — the black people. According to the "Color Bar" Bill, they may no longer compete with whites and coloreds (people of mixed race) for highly-paid jobs. In the future they will be employed mainly in the mines and factories as unskilled laborers. Women will only find work as domestic servants or nursery maids. Africans cannot vote, so they have no legal way of changing this situation.

TUNNEY BEATS DEMPSEY

Sept. 23, Philadelphia Thousands watched and cheered as the fighting marine, Gene Tunney, pounded Jack Dempsey in ten rounds of fighting. Tunney was given the world heavyweight boxing title in a decision. Dempsey has been away from boxing and has been living in luxury for three years. He was not well prepared for this fight. "I have no alibis to offer," said Dempsey afterwards. Tunney gave high praise to Dempsey, and said, "I have never fought a harder socker."

Tunney going down for the count.

NEWS IN BRIEF . . .

MARY CASSATT DEAD AT 81

June 14, Paris Artist Mary Cassatt, the only American to exhibit her paintings with the French Impressionists, is dead. Mary Cassatt is famous for her paintings of mothers and their children in everyday activities. She was born in western Pennsylvania, and studied at the Pennsylvania Academy of Fine Arts. She settled in Paris and became a close friend of the great painter Edgar Degas.

WILL ROCKETS FLY THROUGH SPACE?

March 16, Washington A rocket enthusiast, Dr. Robert Goddard, has built his own rockets and flown them from the back of an old truck for some time. They were about 3 feet tall, and farmers complained that they landed in their fields! He has now sent one high into the atmosphere from a metal platform. Other scientists point out that, as far as we know, there is no air in space. A rocket would not be able to fly to the moon through a vacuum. Time will tell if Dr. Goddard is right.

BURIED CITY FOUND

Feb. 10, Yucatán Members of an American expedition that has been exploring the jungle here have made an amazing discovery. They have found a buried Mayan city. The site has six temples and twelve other buildings. Most are in fair condition. Archaeologists believe this was a great trading city.

GARBO CAPTIVATES

February, Los Angeles A new actress, Swedish Greta Garbo, has won the hearts of American audiences with the release of her first movie here, *The Torrent.*

HYSTERICS AFTER STAR'S DEATH

Aug. 25, Los Angeles Rudolph Valentino, the star of romantic movies such as *The Sheikh* (1921), died last week of appendicitis. He was only 31. The handsome actor had thousands of fans. Many young ladies are in mourning, and one young dancer has even poisoned herself. Thirty thousand people went to his funeral.

FOOTBALL BRANDED IMMORAL

April 25, Washington The American Association of University Professors reported today that the game of college football promotes immoral behavior.

HOUDINI WAS UNPREPARED FOR SHOCK

Oct. 31, Detroit The entertainer Harry Houdini is dead. He told a group of students that his stomach muscles could take the strongest punches. One of them hit him hard when he was unprepared, and burst his appendix. Houdini drew huge audiences by his "magic" escapes from trunks locked and tied with ropes. Often he would be chained, too. His latest trick was to stay under water for 91 minutes with air that would last only about 6 minutes.

Get out of that! Harry Houdini the escapologist in his heyday.

1927

CHINA

CHIANG KAI-SHEK OPPOSES CHINA'S WARLORDS

Jan. 31, Shanghai   General Chiang Kai-shek, leader of the Chinese Nationalists, is winning China's long civil war. Soldiers of his enemies, the powerful "warlords" of the north, are deserting in thousands. They are joining the Nationalist army, which is now near Shanghai.

THE NATIONALISTS CAPTURE SHANGHAI

April 21, Shanghai   General Chiang Kai-shek's army has entered Shanghai, China's richest port. Factory workers and dockworkers in the city, led by Communist trade union officials, had already overcome all opposition. The Nationalists hardly had to fire a single shot to gain control of the city.

Chiang Kai-shek greeted at Hankow.

THE NATIONALISTS TURN ON THE COMMUNISTS

April 30, Shanghai   Chiang Kai-shek and his leaders have turned against the Communists. Nationalist troops have been hunting them down and brutally killing them. Thousands of workers in Shanghai, who only last week helped the Nationalists gain the city, have been massacred.

THE COMMUNISTS ARE IN HIDING

Dec. 31, China   A leader in the Communist party, Mao Tse-tung, is in hiding in the hills of central China. He has been involved in several failed uprisings. There are less than 10,000 Communists left in China, but they refuse to give in.

NOTED MUSICIAN IN HARLEM

Dec. 4, New York   Duke Ellington, talented composer and musician, is in town. He and his band have started what should be a long and exciting engagement at Harlem's Cotton Club.

WHY THE COPS CAN'T CATCH THE ROBBERS

July, Chicago   Besides selling alcohol illegally, Chicago's gangsters are forcing money from small businesses by "protection." Each week they demand money from shopkeepers or garage owners. If they refuse, their business premises may be mysteriously destroyed. Top gangster Al Capone is proving hard to arrest because, it is said, he has friends in city government.

FAME FOR PILOT OF THE *SPIRIT OF ST. LOUIS*

June 13, New York Mr. Charles Lindbergh rode through the streets of New York today like a conquering hero. His name is known to everyone because of his nonstop flight across the Atlantic last month. His one-engined plane, the *Spirit of St. Louis*, contained neither radio, parachute, nor map. During the whole 33½-hour journey he had to rely on his eyes and his sense of direction. When he landed in Paris he had traveled 3,600 miles (5,800 km).

As his motorcade drove through New York today, office workers made paper streamers from old files and phone books and showered them down from their skyscraper windows. Mr. Lindbergh has received 3½ million fan letters!

Mr. Charles Lindbergh, the solo pilot.

The start of the historic flight as the *Spirit of St. Louis* takes off from Long Island.

NEWS IN BRIEF . . .

NEW BREATHING DEVICE

August, Boston Philip Drinker and Louis Shaw of Harvard are hoping to complete the development of their "iron lung" shortly. This machine will help people with paralyzed chest muscles to breathe, and should benefit polio victims.

BABE RUTH IS A WINNER

Sept. 30, New York Baseball champion "Babe" Ruth has scored a record 60 home runs in this season, which started in April. Ruth is the best left-handed pitcher in the American League. The New York Yankees bought him from the Boston Red Sox in 1913. Since then the Yankees have been very successful.

Babe Ruth dressed for action.

THE TALKIES ARE HERE

Oct. 6, Hollywood The release of Al Jolson's new movie, *The Jazz Singer*, is a special event. The songs he sings come from a special sound track attached to the moving pictures. But the most amazing thing is that, for the first time, you can actually hear his voice speaking. "You ain't heard nothing yet," he drawls.

Motion pictures will soon be showing other talkies. Greta Garbo and Conrad Veidt are two "silent" stars who are hastily learning English.

TOP DESIGNER FASHIONS

Spring, London Dress designers are full of ideas this year. Worth has put the waist back above the hips. His hemline comes just below the knee, though his evening wear reaches the calf. A new designer, Elsa Schiaparelli, introduces more casual wear for daytime. Her short pleated skirts and lightweight sweaters are bought by fashion-conscious ladies who also want comfort. Norman Hartnell favors longer skirts for his models.

YEHUDI MENUHIN, A YOUNG MUSICIAN TO WATCH

Feb. 13, Paris An 11-year-old American violinist, Yehudi Menuhin, is delighting audiences here. At his first European concert he played a Tchaikovsky violin concerto. This little blond boy asked the leader of the orchestra to tune his violin for him. And when a string broke halfway through, he waited calmly while the leader fitted a new one. Yehudi Menuhin started to learn the violin when he was four. Two years later he played at a Young People's Concert in San Francisco. Critics say he is a remarkable player and has a great future ahead of him.

GOOD-BYE TO THE TIN LIZZIES

Dec. 1, Detroit Mr. Henry Ford is going to stop making Model T cars. Over the last 20 years about 15 million "Tin Lizzies" have been sold. Ford's slogan was, "You can have any color you like, as long as it's black." Ford's rival, General Motors, is now producing cars in a range of colors. Their cars have six cylinders and modern hydraulic brakes. From today, Ford's Model T will be replaced by the Model A, with a self-starter and shock absorbers, and fitted with an unbreakable windshield.

1928

HARD TIMES IN RUSSIA
TROTSKY IS IN DISGRACE

Jan. 16, Moscow A few years ago, Leon Trotsky was a hero. He was one of the leaders of the Russian Revolution. But Stalin forced Trotsky to give up control of the Red Army and dismissed him from the Communist party. Now Trotsky has been moved to a prison in the loneliest part of the country. Trotsky is one of 30 Soviet leaders arrested on Stalin's orders.

WORKERS ARE BLAMED FOR POOR ECONOMY

Oct. 1, Moscow Stalin wants to make the USSR a technically advanced country. The new Dnieper Dam will supply electricity. The power plant at the dam will be the largest in the world.

Stalin has a large force of secret police. They told him that coal miners were holding back production. Of the 52 miners brought to trial, five have been executed. Nobody knows whether they were really guilty, or forced to make a confession.

STALIN MUST BE OBEYED

Sept. 30, Moscow Many Bolshevik leaders are alarmed at the way Stalin is running the country, but they dare not say so. Only one critic has spoken out. Nikolai Bukharin has published an article in *Pravda* defending the peasants and farmers. Stalin is not likely to allow him to go unpunished.

CHIANG KAI-SHEK HEADS NORTH
CHINESE AND JAPANESE CLASH

May 11, Shantung province Chinese Nationalist troops under General Chiang Kai-shek have marched north and entered Tsinan, a town where 2,000 Japanese civilians are living. When 11 of these civilians were killed by Nationalist soldiers, the Japanese government sent troops to protect its people. The Japanese general demanded that Chinese officers should be publicly punished for the killings. Chiang Kai-shek refused, and so the Japanese attacked and killed over a thousand Chinese soldiers. The rest were forced out of the city. They joined other sections of Chiang's army, which is marching towards Peking.

Joseph Stalin, the new strong man in Russia.

NATIONALISTS REACH THEIR GOAL

June 4, Peking The Nationalists captured Peking today, after its governor was killed as he fled to Manchuria. Peking has been the capital city, and the home of China's emperors, for 900 years. There is no longer an emperor, but it was necessary for the Nationalists to capture such an important town. However, the new capital is to be at Nanking, in central China. Chiang Kai-shek will be China's first president.

IS THE NEW IMMIGRANT A PRINCESS?

Feb. 6, New York Ever since Tsar Nicholas II of Russia and his family were murdered in 1918 by the Bolsheviks, there have been rumors about their deaths. Americans are now wondering if one of the royal children survived the massacre. A young woman arrived in New York today. She claims that she is the Tsar's youngest daughter, Princess Anastasia. Many people are doubtful. It seems unlikely that the Bolsheviks would have allowed a member of the royal family to escape.

MILLIONS HEAR NATIONWIDE BROADCAST

Jan. 5, New York The National Broadcasting Company last night connected all 48 states to broadcast a radio program with entertainers who were actually hundreds of miles apart. Will Rogers broadcast from his Beverly Hills home. He then introduced Al Jolson. Jolson sang ''California, Here I Come'' from New Orleans. Paul Whiteman's orchestra played from New York, and Fred and Dorothy Stone sang from Chicago.

ANOTHER "FIRST" FOR WOMEN AT THE OLYMPICS

Aug. 12, Amsterdam Women competed for the first time in track events at this year's Olympic Games in the Netherlands. Germany also took part, for the first time since the war, and sent 300 athletes.

Paavo Nurmi of Finland, who did so well in 1924, added one more gold and two silver medals to his collection. Hockey is back in the games, and India was the winner. Its team scored 29 goals altogether, and none of its opponents scored at all.

The victorious Indian hockey team in action.

AMELIA EARHART FLIES ATLANTIC

June 18, New York When the plane landed in Carmarthenshire, South Wales, today, Amelia Earhart became the first woman passenger to fly the Atlantic. She did it because, "When one is offered such a tremendous adventure it would be too inartistic to refuse it . . . . I knew the moment this chance came to me that if I turned it down, I would never forgive myself." Miss Earhart said that even when motors spat and gas ran low, she never doubted success.

PUERTO RICAN LEADER STABBED

June 18, San Juan, Puerto Rico Antonio Barcelo, president of the Puerto Rican senate, was stabbed today. Justo Matos, 35 years old, and believed to be mentally unbalanced, attacked Señor Barcelo with a chisel. The chisel made a four-inch wound. It was then turned aside by a rib. It is not known whether Señor Barcelo will live. Matos himself was shot by a bystander who was not identified. It is not known whether his wound is fatal.

POLAR EXPLORER KILLED

June 20, Spitzbergen, Norway The Norwegian explorer, Roald Amundsen, died today when his seaplane crashed into the Arctic Ocean. He was trying to rescue a fellow explorer, who has been stranded on the ice for a month after his airship was forced to land. Two years ago the two friends were the first people to fly over the North Pole. In 1911, Amundsen achieved his highest goal: his expedition was the first to reach the South Pole on foot — 30 days ahead of the British explorer Captain Robert F. Scott.

NEWS IN BRIEF . . .

LOUIS IS KING OF THE JAZZ AGE

July 20, Chicago Jazz has conquered America, and nowhere is it better played than in Chicago. Here Louis Armstrong ("Satchmo") plays trombone or cornet, and sings to his band's music. Armstrong's Hot Five play brilliant solo passages. They are also famous for their "scat" singing, rapid, meaningless "de-doo-be-doo" words, and for slowing up or quickening the beat. Their latest record, is "West End Blues." Jazz is very popular with the young.

LAND SPEED RECORD

Feb. 19, Florida Malcolm Campbell, the well-known racing driver, has beaten the land speed record in the specially built *Bluebird*. Over two laps, on the racing track at Daytona, he averaged a speed of 214.8 mph.

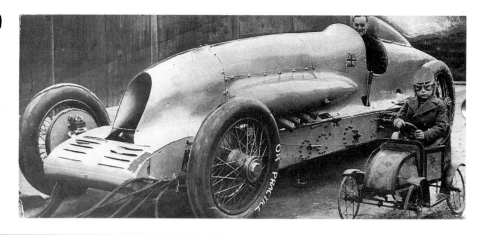

Malcolm Campbell in *Bluebird*. His son Donald is in the pedal car.

ETNA ERUPTS

Nov. 12, Sicily Molten lava is pouring down the slopes of the volcano Mount Etna toward the town of Catania, between the mountain and the Mediterranean Sea. Mount Etna erupted a week ago, and since then the lava has overwhelmed villages and crops on the mountain slopes. The townspeople of Catania are afraid that if it continues, their homes will be in danger. People living in this region are used to small eruptions, but this is one of the largest ever recorded. The erupting volcano glows red at night and is an amazing sight.

This famous volcano on the eastern coast of the island of Sicily is 11,122 feet (3,390 m) high. Its first recorded eruption took place in 700 B.C. In 1669, an earthquake occurred at the same time as an eruption. About 20,000 people were killed in that disaster.

MICKEY MOUSE, MOVIE STAR, SPEAKS

Nov. 18, Hollywood Walt Disney's funny cartoon character Mickey Mouse first starred in *Plane Crazy* earlier this year. That was a silent movie. Today you can see — and hear — Mickey in the talkie *Steamboat Willie*.

FLYING DOCTORS

May, Sydney, Australia To cover the vast territory of the "outback," an Australian doctor came up with a new idea: he bought a plane and hired a pilot to take him to his patients. Other doctors have followed his example and they have formed the Flying Doctor Service.

ENTER POOH AND PIGLET AGAIN

Oct. 11, London Mr. A.A. Milne has published a second children's book, *The House at Pooh Corner*. It continues the story of Christopher Robin, Pooh, and all the other animals we have met already in *Winnie-the-Pooh*. Mr. Milne has also written two books of poetry for children.

1929

FALL OF THE MIGHTY DOLLAR
SHARE PRICES ARE RISING RAPIDLY

Sept. 3, New York Fewer houses have been built this year, and fewer cars sold. The American economy may be slowing down. In spite of this, our new President, Mr. Herbert Hoover, hailed this year as one of "happiness and hopefulness." For many Americans, happiness means wealth, and the creation of even more wealth by buying stocks and shares. Today on Wall Street, the American Stock Exchange, sold a record number of shares. The price of all shares is still rising. Those who have sold shares recently have made their fortunes.

"BLACK TUESDAY" AS STOCK MARKET FALLS

Oct. 24, New York Last Thursday share prices began to fall dramatically. People panicked and tried to sell their shares. Brokers (dealers) were unable to cope with all the customers. As thousands of shares were sold, the price fell even further. More and more people tried to get their money back. The result of this was that even more shares were sold — and so the decline went on.

When the stock market opened this morning, traffic came to a standstill as thousands of investors blocked the road. They were trying to push their way into the Stock Exchange, to sell shares that had become almost worthless. After 16 million shares had been sold, prices dropped to rock bottom. There is an air of disbelief in America tonight. Many investors face ruin.

A ruined investor makes a desperate attempt to raise money after the Wall Street crash.

AFTER THE CRASH

Dec. 31, New York With businesses becoming bankrupt every day, the number of unemployed has risen to over three million. There are no bank loans available because the banks are also in great difficulties. Some people have committed suicide rather than face the loss of all their property, and huge debts which they could not pay. This is an unhappy end to the decade. Americans are slowly realizing that the boom years of prosperity are over.

THE SMALLEST STATE IN THE WORLD

Feb. 11, Rome Today the pope and Benito Mussolini have ended a long disagreement between the Church and the Italian government. In the future the pope's palace, the Church of St. Peter, and all the great buildings nearby, will form a separate state. It will be called Vatican City. The pope will be its ruler, and the Italian government will have no control over its affairs. Mussolini promises that all schools in Italy will teach the Catholic faith.

GANGSTERS KILLED ON ST. VALENTINE'S DAY

Feb. 14, Chicago The war between rival gangs came to a climax today. Al Capone's gang, dressed as policemen, raided a garage where a rival gang was waiting for delivery of illegal alcohol. They lined the men up against a wall, then opened fire with machine guns and killed them all. But the leader of the gang, Bugsy Moran, was not in the garage. Though Bugsy has lost half his men, his sideline is flourishing: he supplies expensive wreaths for gangsters' funerals!

HELP ARRIVES FOR FARMERS

Aug. 11, Washington President Hoover today signed the Agricultural Marketing Act, which creates a Federal Farm Board. The Board will encourage the founding of farm cooperatives and will try to stabilize prices of farm products. Mr. Hoover hopes the new law will help the farmers, who have been in serious financial trouble.

FIRST ACADEMY AWARDS HELD

May 16, Hollywood The first annual awards of the Academy of Motion Picture Arts and Sciences were presented at a banquet at the Hollywood Roosevelt Hotel. Janet Gaynor, a newcomer, won for three of her movies, and Emil Jannings for two of his. The movie *Wings* won best picture. The founders of the Academy hope to give the movie industry a more dignified image. At the end of the evening Al Jolson said, "I can use one (referring to the statuette presented to winners). I need another paperweight."

MUSTAFA KEMAL REFORMS TURKEY

Dec. 31, Constantinople In only six years, Mustafa Kemal has made Turkey into an efficient modern state. The Turkish language is now written in Roman and not Arabic script. Education and the legal system are no longer controlled by Islamic teachers and lawyers. No man may have more than one wife. And the red fez, which every man in Turkey wore, is no longer worn — by law.

Arabic and new Roman shop signs in Constantinople.

NEWS IN BRIEF . . .

LIVING APART BY LAW

May, Pretoria, South Africa The South African government has decided to have separate schools and housing areas for Africans and Europeans. They argue that the two races have different cultures. Africans see this as an attempt to keep them less well educated and in inferior jobs.

THE TREASURE SEEKERS

June 27, Italy Gold and silver valued at more than five million dollars was lost when the liner *Egypt* sank in the Atlantic in 1922. Many salvage crews have tried to recover the treasure, but none has succeeded because the wreck is 142 yards (130 meters) deep. Today Signor Aristide Franceschi has become the first diver ever to reach this depth. He stayed under water for nearly two hours. In spite of this effort, Franceschi did not see any sign of the wreck.

Gabrielle "Coco" Chanel.

GERMAN AND BRITISH AIRSHIPS' HISTORIC FLIGHTS

Oct. 14, London The largest airship ever built, the *R101*, made its first flight today. It can carry about 50 passengers. This is Britain's answer to the German *Graf Zeppelin*, which recently completed its round-the-world flight, taking 21½ days. It stopped only three times on this enormous journey. Zeppelins were designed by the German count Ferdinand Zeppelin.

The *R101* airship by London's Tower Bridge.

DRESS SENSE

Spring, Paris To go with the new short hairstyle called the Eton crop, French designer Coco Chanel has introduced a collection of smart, practical clothes in wool jersey. She uses plain pastel colors or stripes and dresses up the simple lines with costume jewelry and beads. Chanel says, "I make fashions that women can breathe in, feel comfortable in, and look good in." Designer Elsa Schiaparelli is so successful that she employs about 2,000 people in her 26 workrooms.

AMERICAN ARTISTS TO EXHIBIT AT NEW MUSEUM

Dec., New York The Museum of Modern Art opened its doors last month with an exhibit of Impressionist art. On the last day of the exhibit, over 5,000 people moved through the Fifth Ave. galleries to admire works by Van Gogh, Gauguin, Seurat, and Cezanne. The new museum, a nonprofit educational institution, was criticized for not including works by Americans. The next exhibit will show several paintings by Americans Georgia O'Keefe, Max Weber, and Edward Hopper.

PEOPLE OF THE TWENTIES

Amelia Earhart, pilot 1897–1937?

Amelia Earhart was born in Atchison, Kansas. She was the first woman passenger to cross the Atlantic Ocean by air, the first woman to pilot a plane across it alone, the first woman to cross the United States in both directions by air, and the first woman to receive the Distinguished Flying Cross. On her first transatlantic flight, in 1928, she flew from Newfoundland to Wales. In writing a book about the experience, she met and married her publisher, George Putnam. In 1937, Earhart tried to fly around the world. Her plane vanished in the Pacific Ocean and no authenticated trace of her was ever found.

F. Scott Fitzgerald, writer 1896–1940

F. Scott Fitzgerald was the historian of America's Jazz Age, the Roaring Twenties. He and his wife Zelda were leading players in the high life he described in his collections of short stories and in his novels. His first novel, *This Side of Paradise*, and another, *The Beautiful and the Damned*, created a great deal of interest. However, his continuing literary importance rests largely on his novel *The Great Gatsby*, which exposed the moral emptiness of American high life. Fitzgerald's early success led to an extravagant life-style, which probably damaged his literary output.

Charlie Chaplin, actor and director 1889–1977

As a boy in London, Chaplin learned his comedy acting in the music halls. He was invited to Hollywood in 1913 by the Keystone film studio. Here he invented the character of the sad little tramp. In the 1920s he was directing great comedies such as *The Kid* and *The Gold Rush*. When talking pictures arrived, Chaplin ignored them: *City Lights* (1931) and *Modern Times* (1936) were both silent comedies. During World War II he directed and starred in *The Great Dictator*, which made fun of Hitler and the Nazis.

Paul Robeson, actor and singer 1898–1976

Paul Robeson, an American actor, singer, and political activist, was the son of a former slave. At Rutgers University, Robeson was elected to Phi Beta Kappa, the national honor society. He began his successful career in the 1920s. He was recognized around the world for his fine performances in such plays as *Othello* and *The Emperor Jones*. Conservatives opposed his work for peace, racial equality, and better labor conditions; and also his friendship with the Soviet Union.

Mustafa Kemal, Turkish leader 1881–1938

Kemal was born to poor parents but was very successful in his army career and rose to head a government in Ankara, Turkey, when the British occupied Constantinople after World War I. He deposed the sultan and reformed the government. He made sweeping changes in Turkey's legal system and schools. He completely changed the country's outlook, to bring it into line with modern European society. He discouraged Turkish men from wearing their traditional wide trousers and brimless hat known as a "fez." He became known as Kemal Atatürk, "father of the Turks."

Albert Schweitzer, humanitarian 1875–1965

The brilliant Albert Schweitzer was born in Germany. He was a musician, clergyman, philosopher, physician, missionary, and writer. Before Schweitzer was 30, he had a worldwide reputation as a writer on religion, an organist, an interpreter of the works of Johann Sebastian Bach, and an authority on Bach's life. He studied medicine from 1905 to 1913 and became a medical missionary. His hospital in Lambaréné in French Equatorial Africa (now Gabon) treated many thousands of Africans yearly. A great humanitarian, Schweitzer is probably most famous for his work among lepers. In 1923, he completed the first two volumes of his influential book *The Philosophy of Civilization*. Other works include *The Quest of the Historical Jesus* (1906) and *Out of My Life and Thought* (1931).

Greta Garbo, movie star 1905–1990

Greta Garbo was born in Sweden. She won a scholarship to drama school and was picked out by a leading film director as a future star. He took her to Hollywood, where her acting ability brought her into the limelight. Greta Garbo was a very private person, and she avoided publicity. Her fame rests on only a few films, from the early days of Hollywood. When talking pictures were introduced, she learned English, but she never lost her Swedish accent. At the age of 36 she left Hollywood and never made another film.

Albert Einstein, physicist 1879–1955

Albert Einstein, born in Germany, was a genius who made many scientific discoveries that have changed the way in which scientists work.

By the age of 36 one of his discoveries had won him the Nobel Prize for Physics (1921). This discovery has to do with the effect of colored light on electrons. His Theory of Relativity states that "all motion is relative." It says that matter can be turned into energy. This is the principle behind the atomic bomb.

When Hitler came to power, Einstein, who was Jewish, became an American citizen. Up until the time of his death he was working on ways to control the energy of the atom.

American Firsts

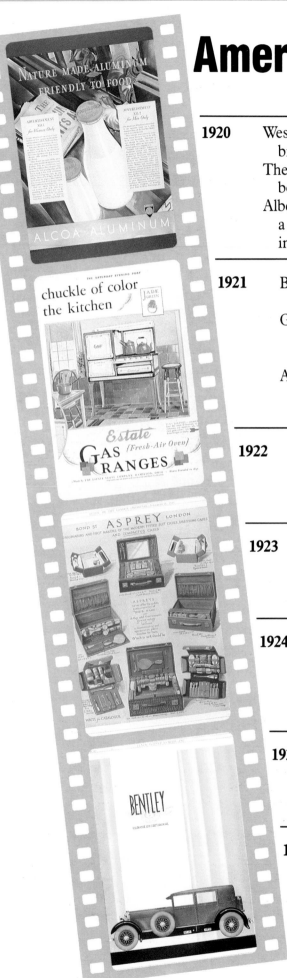

1920 Westinghouse opened the first American broadcasting station, in Pittsburgh, Penn.
The first transcontinental airmail run was made between New York and California.
Albert Michaelson made the first measurement of a star, using the interferometer he had invented in 1880.

1921 Biologist Thomas H. Morgan described the chromosome theory of heredity.
George Washington Carver, African-American scientist, lectured a congressional committee on the many uses of peanuts.
Alice Robertson of Oklahoma was the first woman to preside over the House of Representatives.

1922 The first mechanical switchboard was installed, in the New York City telephone system.
The first commercial was broadcast over WEAF, in New York City.

1923 Colonel Jacob Schick patented the electric razor.
Lieutenant R.L. Maughan set a world's record for airplane speed at 233.87 miles per hour.
Time magazine was published for the first time.

1924 The Radio Corporation of America demonstrated the first wireless transmission of photos, from London to New York City.
The U.S. finished 4th overall in the first winter Olympics, held in Chamonix, France.

1925 George F. and Gladys H. Dick formulated an antitoxin for scarlet fever.
Prest-Air Devices Co., Long Island City, N.Y., made the first commercial dry ice.

1926 Robert H. Goddard fired the first successful liquid-fueled rocket.
The Book-of-the-Month Club was organized, revolutionizing bookselling.
The first transatlantic radiotelephone conversation was demonstrated.

1927 John D. Rust invented a mechanical cotton picker.

The Holland Tunnel, connecting New Jersey and Manhattan Island under the Hudson River, opened to traffic.

1928 George Eastman demonstrated the first color motion pictures, in Rochester, N.Y.

Walt Disney first introduced Mickey Mouse, in the cartoon *Plane Crazy*.

The first animated electric sign in the U.S. was mounted, in Times Square, New York City.

1929 Commercial production of frozen foods begun by Postum Company, using Clarence Birdseye's process for fast freezing.

Lieutenant James Doolittle made the first airplane flight using instruments only to guide the plane.

New words and expressions

The English language is always changing. New words are added to it, and old words are used in new ways. Here are a few of the words and expressions that first appeared or first came into popular use in the 1920s:

ambivalence	high-hat
banana split	hitchhiker
beautician	insulin
blue chip	I.Q.
broadcast	jaywalk
case the joint	jeepers
cockamamie	jitters
dinette	jive
double feature	leftist
drugstore cowboy	license plate
Eskimo pie	luncheonette
fascist	mad money
filling station	nitwit
fine-tune	on the ropes
gang-up	palooka
garbage truck	perm
gate-crasher	pin the blame
gigolo	smoke-filled room
gimmick	sports page
grease monkey	take it

How many of these words and expressions do we still use today? Do you know what they all mean?

Glossary

Bolsheviks: members of the original Russian Communist political party.

diabetic: A person whose body does not absorb sugar properly. A hormone called insulin is used to control this condition.

embalm: to preserve after death with special ointments.

erupt: to blow up (volcano), throwing out rocks and lava.

Fascists: Italian anti-Communist political party.

flapper: a young woman in the 1920s, whose behavior was considered free and unconventional.

general strike: strike in which workers in many industries join to support the original strikers.

impeach: to charge a government official with wrongdoing in office.

indict: to charge with a crime.

lava: a red-hot liquid. When it cools, it becomes a hard black rock.

mandate: a country given in trust to one of the winning nations after World War I.

mausoleum: a large tomb.

merger: a way of combining two or more business organizations.

motorcade: a line of motorcars in a procession.

picket: to stand outside a workplace to persuade others to respect a strike, or to demonstrate or protest.

Prohibition: the banning of alcohol during the 1920s in the United States.

protectorate: a country under the care or protection of a stronger political unit.

reparations: compensation for war damage.

suffrage: the right to vote.

Further Reading

Blocher, Arlo. *Jazz*. New ed. Troll Assoc, 1976

Brown, Gene. *Duke Ellington*. Silver Burdett Press, 1990

Cairns, Trevor. *Twentieth Century*. Lerner, 1984

Carey, Helen and Greenberg, Judith. *How to Read a Newspaper*. Watts, 1983

Caulkins, Janet. *Joseph Stalin*. Watts, 1990

Cook, Fred J. *The Ku Klux Klan: America's Recurring Nightmare*, Messner, 1989

Emerson, Kathy L. *Making Headlines: A Biography of Nellie Bly*. Macmillan Child Grp, 1989

Haskins, James. *Black Dance in America: A History Through Its People*. Crowell Jr. Bks, 1990

Hunter, Nigel. *The Movies*. Steck-Vaughn, 1990

Migneco, Ronald and Biel, Timothy L. *The Crash of 1929*. Lucent Bks, 1989

Polikof, Barbara G. *Herbert C. Hoover: Thirty-first President of the United States*. Garret Ed, 1990

Randolph, Blythe. *Charles Lindbergh*. Watts, 1990

Samuels, Steven. *Paul Robeson*. Chelsea House, 1988

Smith, Betsy C. *Women Win the Vote*. Silver Burdett Press, 1989

Stevens, Rita. *Calvin Coolidge: Thirtieth President of the United States*. Garrett Ed, 1990

Index